Pandas

Pandas

by Susan Kueffner

Reader's Digest

Published by The Reader's Digest Association, Inc.

London • New York • Sydney • Montreal

CONTENTS

Chapter 1

On the bamboo trail

DID YOU KNOW?

A panda does not have a permanent den. Instead, it takes shelter in trees and caves that it comes upon as it looks for food.

'Grrrrr!' The sound of a snow leopard echoed through the mountain forest in central China. Blue-nosed golden monkeys scattered high in the trees, and a cuckoo called out. The hungry leopard crouched low to the ground. What was that up ahead? Was it just the snow? Or was something really there?

From a tree limb high above, a giant panda bear watched and waited. An expert climber, the panda had sped up the tree at the first sign of danger. She sat comfortably on the limb without making a sound. The leopard looked up. But the black patches of the panda's coat blended with the dark branches of the tree and the white patches disappeared into the light of the sky. Disappointed and still hungry, the big cat walked on.

In this part of China, the snow continued to fall, but the panda wasn't cold. Her thick fur coat was warm and waterproof. After a time, she climbed down from the tree and continued her search for food. She was hungry too!

She lumbered along slowly, walking pigeon-toed through the misty woods. Soon she came to a steep slope. She climbed up and up, using the hairy pads on her paws to grip the icy mountainside without slipping. From his perch high in a tree, a little red panda watched his cousin make the climb.

What's in a name?

The 5kg red panda, also known as the lesser panda, has lots in common with the giant panda. They share the same habitat, the same bamboo diet and the same name. And both animals are among the most endangered. But scientific tests place the red panda in the raccoon family and the giant panda in the bear family.

DID YOU KNOW?

A panda sits upright to eat, which keeps its front paws free to hold the bamboo and to pluck off the shoots and leaves.

When she got closer to the top of the mountain, the trees were so close together that the panda could only see a little way in front of her. Using her short, powerful legs, she pushed through the tangle of trees and plants. A bamboo rat scurried past. It would have made a nice treat, but the rat was too fast for her to catch. Now the panda was really hungry.

Up ahead, an icy stream blocked her path. But wait! What was that? A tall patch of bamboo was growing on the other side. It was her favourite food! Without hesitating, the panda waded into the icy water and swam across.

The hungry panda broke some stalks and leaves off a bamboo plant and immediately sat down upright in the snow. Gripping the bamboo in her two front paws, she gobbled it all down – stems, twigs and leaves. She continued with the feast, happily munching and crunching on it all for hours.

When she was full, the panda took a little time out for fun. She leaned back and slid down a hill on her back – but head first! Pheasants flew up, startled by her silly play. She climbed back up the hill, pushed a rock down the slope and chased after it, batting it with her paw. A mouse ran for cover, and a bird called, 'Cuckoo! Cuckoo!'

After a while, the panda grew tired. She flopped to the ground and closed her eyes. Soon her hunger pangs would begin again, but for now she would rest. It had been a very busy day.

Chapter 2

The body
of a panda

Even today some scientists believe that the giant panda is so special that it belongs in a family group all its own.

Is the panda a bear?

When European scientists first saw the panda in China, they were sure it was a kind of bear. However, when the first skeleton of a panda was examined at a French natural history museum, the scientists there did not agree. The skull was different, the teeth were different, and it had a wrist bone that acted like a thumb. These scientists thought the panda belonged to the same family as – surprise – the raccoon! This argument went on for more than 100 years, until tests performed in the 1980s showed that the giant panda had the same DNA as a bear.

A spotty story

How did panda bears get their spots? According to a Tibetan myth, the panda was originally an all-white bear. One day a young shepherdess tried to protect a panda cub from being attacked by a leopard. The leopard attacked and killed her instead. All the pandas in the world were so moved by the girl's brave deed that they attended her funeral wearing armbands of black ashes as a sign of respect. As they cried in sorrow, the pandas wiped their eyes, hugged one another and covered their ears to soften the sound of their sobs. The black ashes wiped off on their fur, and the marks have been there ever since.

In reality, the panda's colouring is an example of nature's camouflage. The panda's coat blends into the dark rocks, white snow and light skies of its mountain habitat.

Not so cuddly

Pandas may look as soft and cuddly as teddy bears, but in fact, their thick fur is stiff, coarse and a bit oily. It helps keep out the cold of snowy winters and acts as waterproofing in the rainy climate of the Chinese forests.

A panda has a powerful body with a huge head, massive jaws, strong teeth and short, thick legs. It has a short tail, only about 15cm long, which is hardly ever seen. The tail is hidden away in the panda's fur, protecting the scent glands that are used to attract a mate.

Adult male pandas grow to be about 1.5m long from nose to tail, 75cm high at the shoulder, and can weigh up to 100kg. Females are a bit smaller – about 1.4m long, 60cm high at the shoulder and about 80kg in weight.

Pandas can stand upright, but they can't walk that way. Their short hind legs just aren't strong enough to support their bodies. A panda's bones are twice as heavy as the bones of other animals the same size.

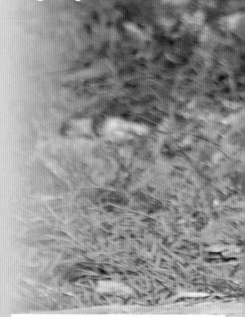

Giant pandas are walkers, not runners. With their weak hind legs, a lumbering trot is about as fast as they can go – and not for very long!

DID YOU KNOW?

Pandas walk on all fours. But they walk with their front paws turned inward, or pigeon-toed.

Despite their bulky bodies, pandas are expert tree climbers. In fact, they can sit for hours on a branch and often even sleep there.

DID YOU KNOW?

Pandas prefer to dine on the delicate shoots and tender leaves of bamboo. But they'll eat the woody stalks if they have to.

Thumbs up

The panda's front paws have special features that help the bear handle bamboo, its food of choice. The five clawed 'fingers' on each paw are lined up in a row, which makes it easy to tear through the bamboo stalks. The front paws also have large wrist bones that act like thumbs. They help the panda to grab and hold on to the green goodies.

Chew on this!

Bamboo is a tall and woody kind of grass. It is often so tough that humans need an axe to cut through it. Imagine trying to bite, chew and swallow it! But it's no problem for pandas, thanks to sharp teeth used for biting and large flat teeth (molars) used for crushing their food. A panda has 42 teeth in all, and its huge jaw muscles are powerful enough to chew through metal. So when it comes to bamboo, pandas are eating machines!

Tough to swallow

A panda has special linings in its throat and stomach that allow it to swallow splintery bamboo stalks without hurting themselves.

Chapter 3

Mothers and cubs

If twin babies are born, only one will survive. A mother panda is not able to care for two babies at one time, and so she must choose the stronger one.

Pandas are shy animals that choose to live most of their lives alone, except in the spring when they look for mates.

Looking for a mate

Scent plays an important part in bringing pandas together to start a family. A six-year-old female panda is fully grown and ready to have a baby. She announces this fact to male pandas by spraying urine and rubbing the scent glands located under her tail against tree trunks and rocks as she makes her way through the forest. Male pandas leave scent marks the same way, letting the female know that they are in her territory. They sniff and follow these scent trails until they eventually find one another.

Bear hugs

A female panda is choosy about her mate. She might turn her back and run, or even climb a tree, to keep away from a male that doesn't appeal to her. She might cuff him with her paw or bite him on the nose! The male might try to change her mind by climbing a tree and calling out a love song of low barks. Sometimes several males will find a single female at the same time. In that case, the female usually chooses the biggest and strongest one.

Most pandas mate sometime between March and May and then go their separate ways.

About five months later, the female will find a den in a hollow tree or cave and give birth to one or two tiny babies.

Tender, loving care

From day one, a mother panda holds her tiny baby close to her body to keep him warm. She never puts her baby down, not even when she sleeps. Just like human babies, baby pandas cry a lot. The mother licks her baby to keep him clean and feeds him milk almost every hour. Mother and cub stay together in the den for two or more weeks. Scientists do not understand exactly how a mother panda can go so long without food.

Finally, when the mother is so hungry that she has to leave the den to look for food, she carries the baby in one of her front paws or in her mouth. While cradling the baby in her paw, she eats bamboo to keep up her strength and continues to feed him milk to help him to grow.

By the end of the first month, the baby panda has all his spots. His eyes only begin to open when he is four to six weeks old, and they aren't fully open until he is seven weeks old. He is still very tiny!

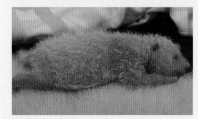

In the pink

A newborn panda is the size of a newborn kitten. This huge bear is only about 15cm long and weighs about 110g when it is born! It has pink skin, a thin coat of white fur, a long tail and no teeth. At birth, its eyes are tightly closed.

DID YOU KNOW?

Mother and child spend lots of time together – cuddling and playing and eating bamboo. In fact, they are constant companions until the cub is about two.

Growing up ... and out!

A baby panda is almost two months old before he weighs 3kg, the weight of an average human newborn baby. He spends much of his day doing just what human babies do – drinking milk. However, a panda can crawl, stand and take his first unsteady steps at three months of age, long before a human baby can do those things. That's when his first teeth appear too.

At three or four months, the panda cub becomes quite playful. He can roll around and climb on his mother's back. At five months, he weighs about 10kg and can walk, trot, climb trees and take his first taste of bamboo. His permanent teeth appear at six months, so he starts eating more solid foods, but he does not stop drinking his mother's milk until he is nine months old. By his first birthday, the baby panda that weighed less than an apple will weigh between 22kg and 36kg!

The following year is spent with his mother – roaming, playing and eating. The baby continues to grow, until he weighs about 100kg at age two. Now fully grown, the young panda leaves his mother for a life of his own. Between the ages of four and eight, he will be ready to mate, and the panda's cycle of life starts again.

Big mama!
A mother panda is about 900 times bigger than her newborn baby!

Chapter 4

The life of a wanderer

One-dish dinners

Surprisingly pandas are carnivores (meat-eaters) by nature, but vegetarians by habit. They'll eat meat if they come across the leftovers of another meat-eating animal, and every now and then will grab fish from a stream. But pandas move too slowly to hunt for 'live food'.

Pandas' favourite food is bamboo. And lots of it! While they will eat many other plants, including mushrooms and flowers and also love honey, these titbits make up only one per cent of their diet. Why? Because bamboo – hundreds of different kinds – is almost always plentiful and easy to find, even in snow. There are few other bamboo-eaters. The only competition comes from the small red panda, a relative of the giant panda, and the bamboo rat.

Unfortunately, there aren't many nutrients in bamboo. The giant panda has to eat between 10kg and 18kg of bamboo every day just to stay alive.

Bamboo plants take years to flower. When they do, they dry, spread their seeds and die. Once or twice a century, a natural disaster strikes and many kinds of bamboo die at the same time. When this happens, there is not enough food for the pandas, and many starve to death.

In the woods

Pandas roam around in the rainy mountain forests of central China at heights ranging from 1,500m to 3,650m. The temperatures there are never too extreme. In the springtime rhododendrons bloom and snow falls in the winter. Grown pandas establish their own territories. This is where they live and look for food. Males wander over larger distances, overlapping the territories of several females. Pandas look for food all the time, but some scientists believe they prefer to roam at twilight or in the dark, sleeping just before dawn and in the afternoon.

At one time scientists believed that the bears went out of their way to avoid each other's company. Recent studies, however, show that pandas overlap each other's home territories and are aware of their neighbours by the scent markings they leave behind.

Unlike other bears that hibernate in winter, pandas are on the move all year long. That's because their food is available year-round and also because they can't eat enough bamboo to fatten up for a long winter's rest. When the weather turns very cold, pandas travel to the warmer valleys. They return to the chillier mountainsides in summer, when the heat is too much for their fur coats.

The panda's Chinese habitat, lush with bamboo the year round, is called the 'bamboo belt'.

Pandas will lie down almost anywhere during the day to take a nap lasting from 15 minutes to 2 hours.

The strong, silent type

There's little need for pandas to develop many different sounds for conversation because they spend most of their time alone. In fact, the quieter they are, the less likely they are to attract attention and the more likely to find the peace and quiet they like.

When they do have something to say, pandas can communicate, but not in ways you might expect. They don't roar like bears. Instead, they bleat – rather like sheep! This is a kind of greeting. They might bark like a dog to attract a mate or make a honking sound when feeling frightened. Young pandas squeal like human babies when they want attention.

Pandas are most likely to make a noisy fuss when they encounter other pandas who are wandering around in their home territory. Then they might huff or growl to warn them to stay away.

DID YOU KNOW?

Panda researchers have counted 11 different panda calls – and four of them are used only when searching for a mate.

Chapter 5

Pandas in the world

Where pandas live

ASIA

EUROPE

China

AFRICA

AUSTRALIA

The **purple** areas show
where pandas live.

People and pandas

Pandas have lived in the world for 2-3 million years. Fossils have been found in Myanmar, Vietnam and China. In ancient China, pandas were thought to have magical and almost divine powers. In fact, the existence of the panda was a secret known by only a few. These rare animals were kept by Chinese emperors, and their prized pelts were given as royal gifts.

The rest of the world only discovered the panda in 1869. That was when a French missionary, who was also a scientist, sent a pelt and skeleton back to a natural history museum in Paris, where it created a sensation. Demand for the beautiful animal sent hundreds of hunters and animal dealers to China to collect skins for museums and live pandas for zoos. Uncontrolled hunting and the cutting down of forests to create farms have made the panda one of the most endangered animals in the world.

Today, there are only about 20 small groups of pandas living in the mountain ranges of three provinces in China: Sichuan, Gansu and Shaanxi. A count conducted by the Chinese government suggests that there are only about 1,000 pandas left in the world.

The future of pandas

The Chinese government considers the panda a national treasure and has taken steps to ensure its survival. The hunting of pandas was outlawed in the 1960s, and logging in the panda's habitat has been banned. The government has also set up protected areas for pandas and has tried to convert some land back to grasslands and forests.

Still, China's population is more than a billion – a million humans for every panda – with 85 million in Sichuan alone, trying to live off the land. The World Wildlife Fund and other groups are working with the government to help farmers to develop businesses, such as ecotourism.

FAST FACTS ABOUT PANDAS

SCIENTIFIC NAME	*Ailuropoda melanoleuca*
CLASS	Mammalia
ORDER	Carnivora
SIZE	Males about 1.5m long from nose to tail; 75cm high at the shoulder
WEIGHT	Males to 100kg Females to 80kg
LIFE SPAN	14 to 20 years in the wild; up to 30 in captivity
HABITAT	Mountain forests in central China

People are working to save this charming creature, who has become the symbol of the World Wildlife Fund and endangered animals everywhere.

GLOSSARY OF WILD WORDS

bamboo	a tropical plant with long, woody, often hollow stems and tender shoots and leaves
camouflage	colours and patterns on an animal that help it to blend in with its surrounding
carnivore	a meat-eating animal
den	place where a wild animal sleeps or rests
DNA	coded material in the cells of living things that determines what they look like and how they act and is passed down to their offspring
ecotourism	travel tours that encourage preservation of areas visited
endangered	a species of plant or animal in danger of extinction

gland	a part of the body that makes chemicals and often releases them, sometimes as a scent		nutrients	the parts of food that help an animal to stay healthy and grow
habitat	the natural environment where an animal or plant lives		pelt	the fur and skin of an animal
			species	a group of living things that are the same in many ways
hibernation	the deep, sleeplike state in which some animals pass the winter		vegetarian	eats only food from plants
mammal	an animal with a backbone and hair on its body that drinks milk from its mother when it is born		wean	to start feeding a baby food other than its mother's milk

INDEX

CREDITS

Pandas is an *All About Animals* fact book
Written by Susan Kueffner

Published in 2011 in the United Kingdom by Vivat Direct Limited (t/a Reader's Digest),
157 Edgware Road, London W2 2HR

Editor: Rachel Warren Chadd
Designer: Nicola Liddiard
Art editor: Simon Webb

Printed in China

ISBN: 978 0 276 44626 9
Book code: 640-035 UP0000-1
Oracle code: 504500042H.00.24